AF413387

I Bloom for Me.

I Shine for Me.

TABLE OF CONTENTS

DEDICATION

This book reflects my own journey to realize true self love; and I dedicate this book to my beautiful soul; the one I rejected for years in favor of the comfort of others. We are not meant to dull our shine for the appeasement of others; we are meant to come to this dimension and move, live, and BE...our own unique expression of 'Love Walking.'

Also inspired by my own experiences of joy and heartbreak; as we first search for love in another; not realizing this attraction is only a mirror for the feelings we need to resolve in ourselves. Every painful relationship is the growth we came here for, and for this I am always grateful.

May we all find our way back to ourselves. We are Love, and we are One.

I FALL IN LOVE WITH ME

I see beauty everywhere

And it is all I want to be

True Beauty
True Joy
True Radiance
True Femininity
True Stillness
True Love

I am these things
I love myself
I am worthy

I am the rose
Budding new flowers
Allowing myself to be vulnerable
Withdrawing my thorns

I am ready to become my deepest desire

I fall in love with ME.

WHAT DOES WATER TASTE LIKE?

Written for My Husband, Michael, for our 7th Wedding Anniversary

Why do I love you?
I could never say a reason
What if that changes or fades
Which true love doesn't do

With life comes many a season
We grow, die, and rebirth
Being beside you along this journey
Means more to me than anything is worth

It's hard for me to say how much I care
Haunted by fear that it will drive you away
But I can write it in words
So, you can look back
Like a post-it note from another time
One of many, I wish I'd saved

And I hope you always know
It's not how you look
It's nothing that can be seen
Only felt when you are near
The essence of you, I can smell you in a breeze
Nothing can cancel you out, my heart floats to you with ease

I see how hard you work
I see how much you care
I SEE how lucky I am to have you
I see more than I can say

The only response
Another question that has no answer,

It can only be felt, tasted, KNOWN for the beauty that it already IS

For who you are, your presence cannot be replicated,
Like a snowflake; you are magic.
Why do I love you…What does Water Taste Like?

7 YEAR ITCH

Written for My Husband, Michael,

That was the year, the best year of our lives

The year our marriage fell apart

Foundations of sand, turned to rock

Two people born anew; instead of searching for new in someone else

A race we learned to take together, then slow it down and make it our own event

I never thought I'd be so happy looking back

So thankful for that year, a new start

Bringing so many truths to the surface

Yes the year our marriage fell apart

And then, rebuilt, on solid rock

To become something real and true

GREATEST SUMMER EVER

It began with an email

A stranger, friend of a friend

Two hearts overtaken

The power of words spoken and mysteries unraveling

Crab hats and belly-laughs

Kid-like fun and x-rated love

Cities moved, a whirlwind romance,

A tune came, like a song known from memory

We didn't think, we just danced

But the song, it never finished

And neither did we

"The Greatest Summer Ever"

Looking back, that's all it was meant to be

THANK YOU

What I didn't know then

It was real love for me

And only suffering for you

Something I wish I could change

If only time and space would allow

You loved me like no one ever had

A love so deep it was unrecognizable to me

A love so sweet

One trying to help me see

But I was blind

By my own self hatred

Pouring onto you and others

I squashed the light that came to restore me

I was operating from a wounded heart

No amount of love you poured into me could fix it

My brokenness came from me

I was on a path of unconsciousness and destruction

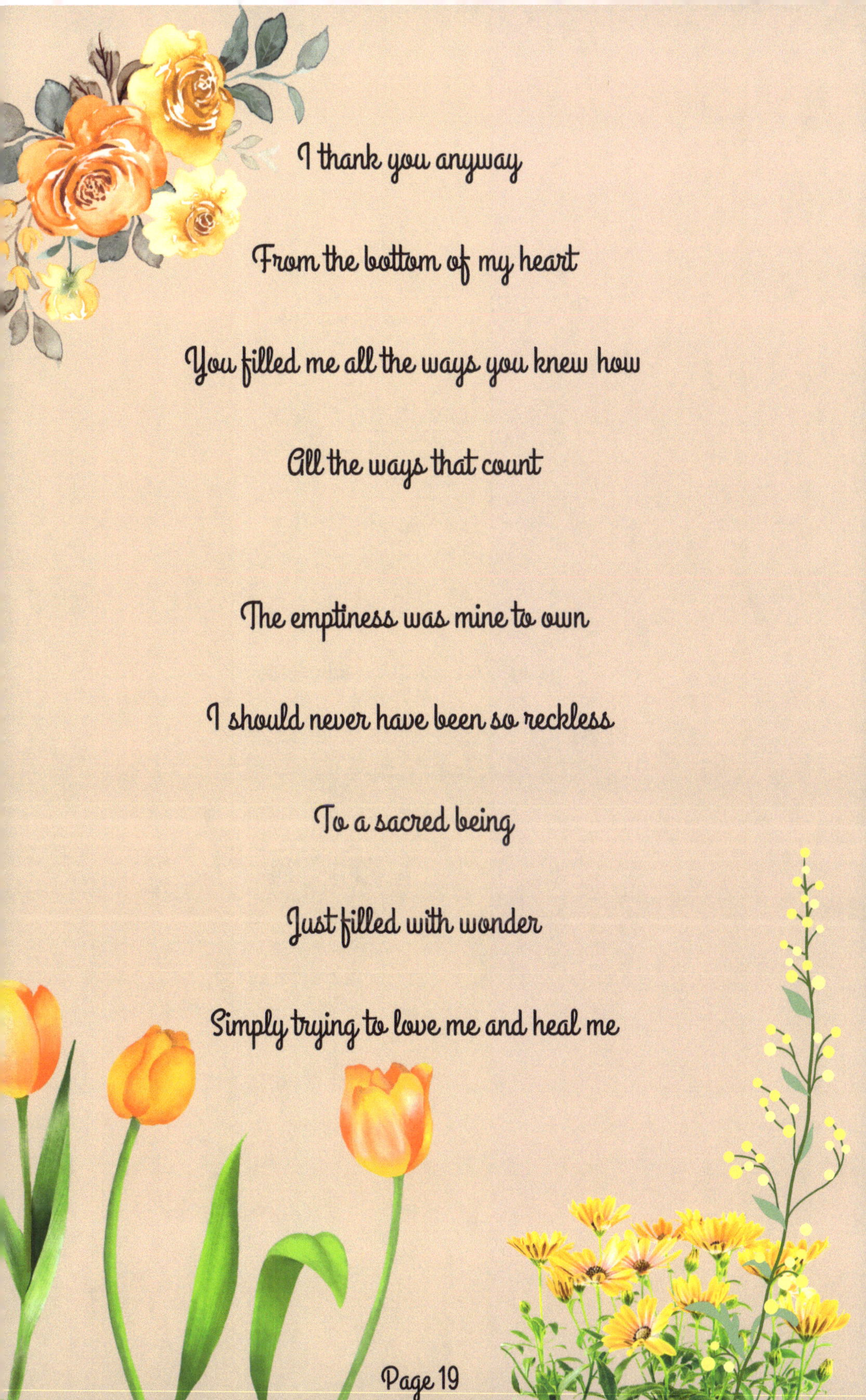

I thank you anyway

From the bottom of my heart

You filled me all the ways you knew how

All the ways that count

The emptiness was mine to own

I should never have been so reckless

To a sacred being

Just filled with wonder

Simply trying to love me and heal me

You saw me, you really saw me

I was your Yellow Bear

You listened, you cared,

You defended me unwavering

I didn't deserve you

But I still THANK YOU

JUST A HAND

The words of my heart will no longer be silent

As I stand here broken by the power of words unheard and wounds unhealed

The countless women told to expect it...
That all men do this and they are just supposed to take it

To give their heart, their spirit away, to just one man
Only to become one of many in the heart and mind of their Beloved

It's just a hand they say

But I say

It's a hand that lovingly that took mine that day

A day I called my happily ever after

A hand….
as an extension of your heart…

your pulse…

your breath of life …
given to another.

Just a hand…

Which wears a ring I placed there, in sacred ceremony and in love

A hand that isn't reaching for mine, caressing my face, hair or body; it reaches for the image of her instead

A hand that resembles his fathers, and our beautiful infant son's….in the ways only a wife and mother would recognize.

It's never just a hand

It's a heart, betrayed

and words of contempt from the man of my dreams
who can't own up to my pain or even hear my words.

He makes empty promises and continues his reckless deeds
that go against the very nature of love.

We create by the power of our thoughts…
As I create love and loyalty with the beauty of mine, he creates lust,
pain, and destruction.

the words stew inside and keep reminding me…
I was never the only one
I was never enough for him

The man I love fully and wholly… loves me only skin deep… as one
of many…he 'loves' me in all the ways that can fade

My whole life is someone else's dream; the appearance of a fairy tale
I wanted the real thing

To be his Beloved

To know the bliss of tender, truth, expressed in the form of love

No, all men don't do this
Boys, little boys do this

It takes a mature heart to have eyes to see and ears to hear
The pain being caused with just his hand.

It's never just a hand
It's my whole heart you held
The whole thing you broke, my whole life you took
Using just your hand.

I WAS NEVER 'THE ONE'

I was never the one

It was never your fault

I did it all, I broke my own heart when it comes down to it

Falling in love with potential

Ignoring actions and pain

Loving you in favor of protection my own heart

Something I'll never do again

euismod lacinia at quis risus sed vulputate odio. Sed
euismod lacinia at quis. Ut tellus elementum
icies lacus sed turpis tincidunt id aliquet
ssa ultricies mi quis. Magna fermen-
us. Eget sit amet tellus cras
vitae et leo duis ut diam
aculis eu non diam phasel-
Cursus sit amet dictum

llamcorper sit amet-
semper feugiat nibh
ing elit duis tris-
mauris nunc
la fames ac
h mauris.
At

BUILT ON SAND

They say things built on sand never last

I thought I was building on sturdy rock,

The rock that binds, the one of marriage, the one that should be true, should be love.

I know the cheesy line, but it is all my heart can fathom to say.

I want to know what love is. I want to know what love actually…IS.

All I know, is that I have never known love, I've only known what's fake, what's false, what can turn on me in an instant.

To know a tender touch, someone who would rather die than cause me an ounce of pain.

To feel a warm embrace with no strings attached; just the desire to exist alongside me,

To know me, in my deepest darkest moments, and to still love me no matter the cost.

Not to fix me; change me, change my words so he can understand me Just. Love. Me.

When confronted with the truth, there was no tears, no remorse, no begging, no I love you's.

Only pleas to see the children, wanting the house, nothing for me, he never wanted me, from the beginning, to the end.

To realize I was never the only one; he never loved me; he never cared; he wanted kids, not a wife;

I was just a role, not a beloved.

Like a princess, kept in a tower, but never freed.

Just a doll, keep playing your part.

The skit is over; the play is cancelled; never to return like a Broadway flop.

The cast departed, only I am left

Which is what I feared all along, losing him

Not realizing how easy it was for me to lose myself

And that …was my biggest and only sin.

FOR SOMEONE ELSE

When the words are afraid to come out, only tears can flow

All the ways I was deceived; all the lies beat at my door

My heart was broken when it was 'just a hand'

Now it is so much more

All the things I wish you'd feel for me, you DO know how to feel them.. and you do want to...

Just for someone else

The actions I wish you'd take, I see that you CAN do all those things… and you enjoy it…

Just for someone else

The date nights I wish you'd plan, I thought it just wasn't your style or it has to be a special occasion…but no, you do like to plan date nights…well wrapped gifts… not for a guilty conscience or obligatory dates…. Just because…just for fun… and
Just for someone else.

The way I wish you'd look at me, like I am the only one who could ever turn your head, I see you can look that way, you can be that excited to hear from someone… or to read her words and actually respond… you can do these things…

Just for someone else.

The way I ache for your touch, yearn for your kind ear and validation, just want you to love me as much as I love you...you do have those desires, you have aches and yearns too..

Just for someone else.

All the ways I dreamt of feeling loved by you, the daydreams of romance that turned real-life...

You have those dreams too I think...

Just with someone else.

You are all I ever wanted, my 'lobster,' my Beloved...

The truth is what I was running from...my feelings not returned;

I was never loved or desired, just seen as a resource

You have what you want from me, but

I was never the one, I was never your choice.

AS A CHILD

I remember thinking love was something out of reach;

How lucky would I be, if the same person I love, would love me back?

Could it be, could I be so lucky, or is that something out of a dream

So many movies share this theme

Guy chases the girl

She resists but eventually her heart sees

No one loves her like him

She puts her guard down;

He breaks down the wall.

That's how it ends,

The Princess finds her Prince Charming after all.

As a child, life was like a movie

I couldn't wait for my happy ending

I had no idea, we are the creators, free will always reigns

And alternate endings may play out instead

GREAT LOVE

Great loves last more than a lifetime

They keep us coming back for more

We hear it's what makes life worth living

What we came all the way here for

The thing about love

Its black and white, yes or no, either it's there or it's not

The flame is hot

Or it won't catch ablaze

Sent out eagerly with love, or

left unreturned; head in a daze

You say I wasn't your great love

It cuts straight like a dagger

Right through my heart

Left broken and tattered

You say I wasn't your great love

I can understand, one day I will be fine

I may not be your great love…

But you… you were mine.

A BAND OF GOLD

The first one lost in the waves, not a day after our vows exchanged

The second one removed, in haste and hate

A woman striving for respect and true love

Hoping to renew her vows, dreaming of how it would be; a fresh start together;

to get to know the person she's loved so many lifetimes, just never the right way.

This time is different; this time love has to win... or so she prays.

She sees the end is near and not from her will or decision

A man never separated from childhood wounds,

seeing enemies where only love grows

He can't see the pain he causes, and willfully ignores the beauty in her heart.

A karmic bond that she saw as sacred, just another lesson in suffering, which she already knows.

Different people, different worlds

One the old ways, one the new

Love just can't unite the two

Like the words of our wedding song, some can part the waters and merge the worlds

I wish that could be our story, the happy ending of my dreams.

Sadly no, it was just a band of gold to him… and like me, something he no longer needs.

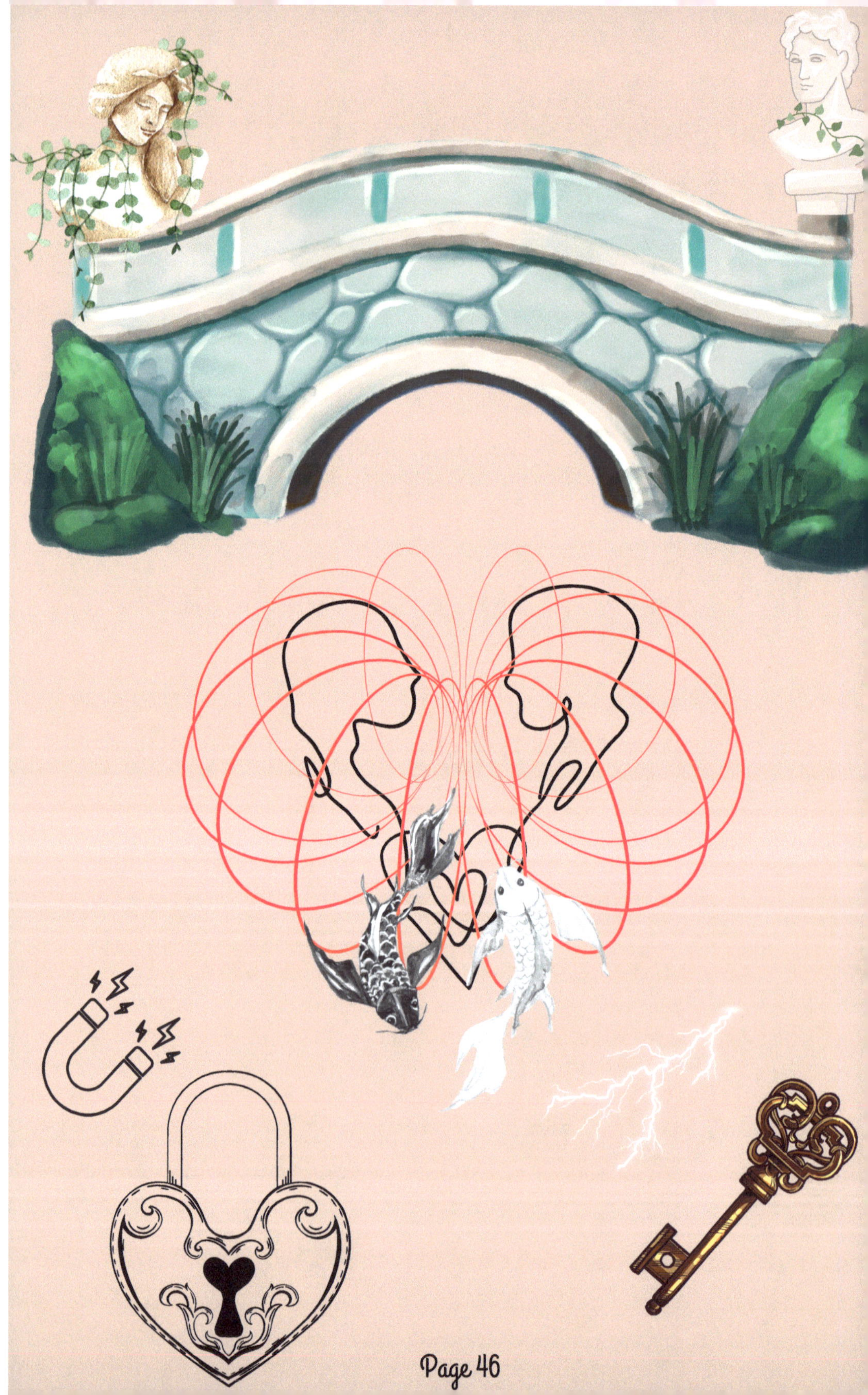

AFTER THE STORM

It's almost more painful
The days without a fight
You get a glimpse of hope
But then the day ends
there's no I love you's
No touching, not even eye contact
And I remember the words he said

He doesn't love me
He admitted
And I said I understand
I'm not mad
And I can't be
All is fair in love and war
You can't blame someone for feelings not returned

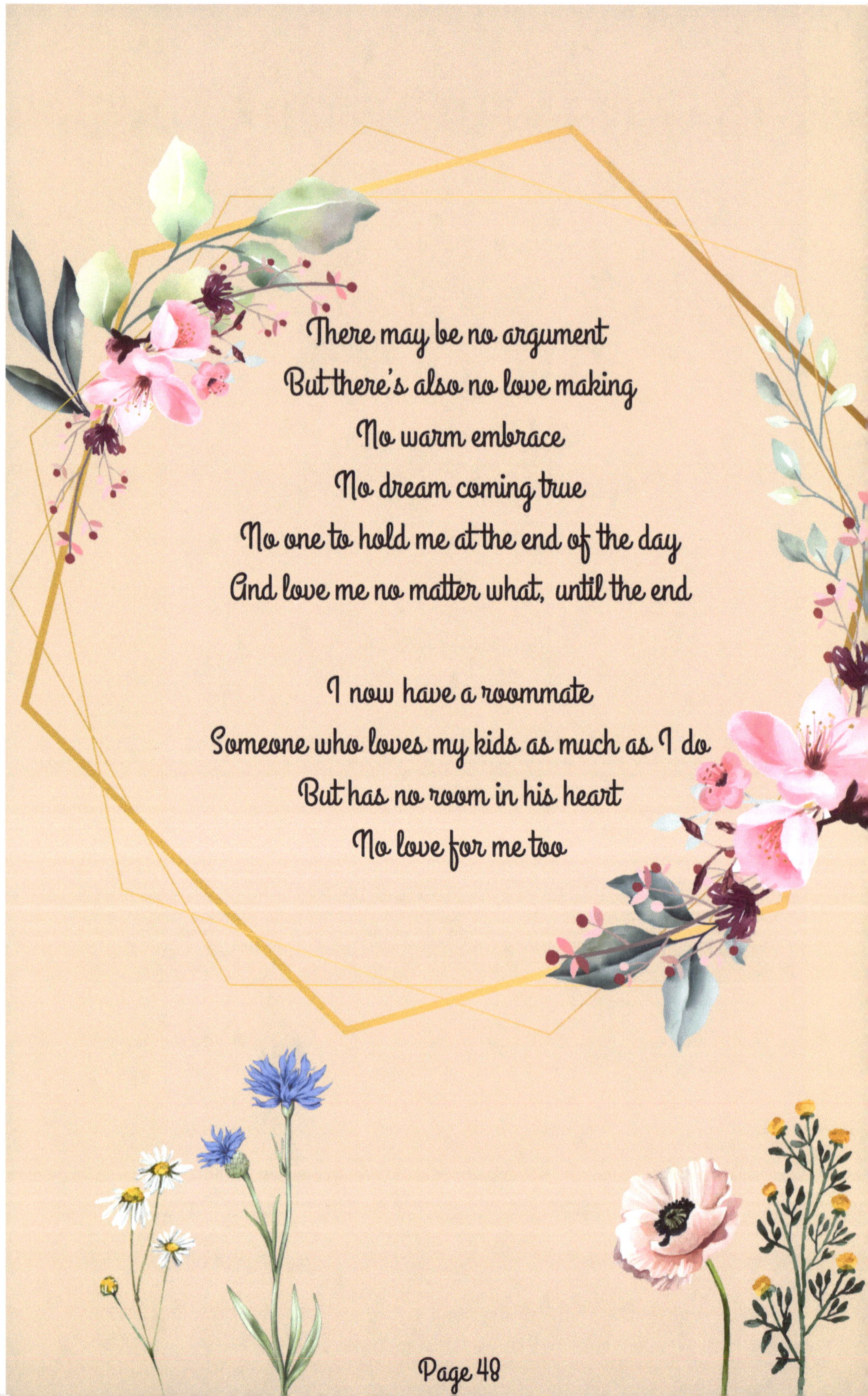

There may be no argument
But there's also no love making
No warm embrace
No dream coming true
No one to hold me at the end of the day
And love me no matter what, until the end

I now have a roommate
Someone who loves my kids as much as I do
But has no room in his heart
No love for me too

LIKE THE ROSE; LIKE THE SPRING

Just because you only see beauty skin deep

Doesn't mean it isn't deeper

Just because you believe lies,

doesn't mean they become true

Just because you tell yourself you were faithful,

Doesn't mean you were

A man who lies to himself will never be truthful to anyone else

The mirror is broken, no longer a reflection of love, but has become a murder weapon instead

Every word I believed was due to my pure heart

Not an ounce of truth in them

But just because you cant see my beauty, doesn't mean its not beaming

The world's beauty escapes you

Your own beauty does too

Like the rose who blooms simply for its own beauty, for its own
purpose and passion

I will keep blooming

Whether you see my beauty or not

It is meant to unfold,

And, like the Spring, it cannot be stopped

I NEVER HAD YOUR HEART

The day we said 'I Do'

Was just an ordinary day to you

But to me, to me, it was the start of my dream come true

The happy ending I couldn't wait to live

My life, my desires, my ability to defend my union

Grew that day

Nothing else mattered to me but us

I thought you were my 'density'… or destiny

And we would find a new way, make a way to each others hearts

Grow deeper and deeper everyday

That was my dream

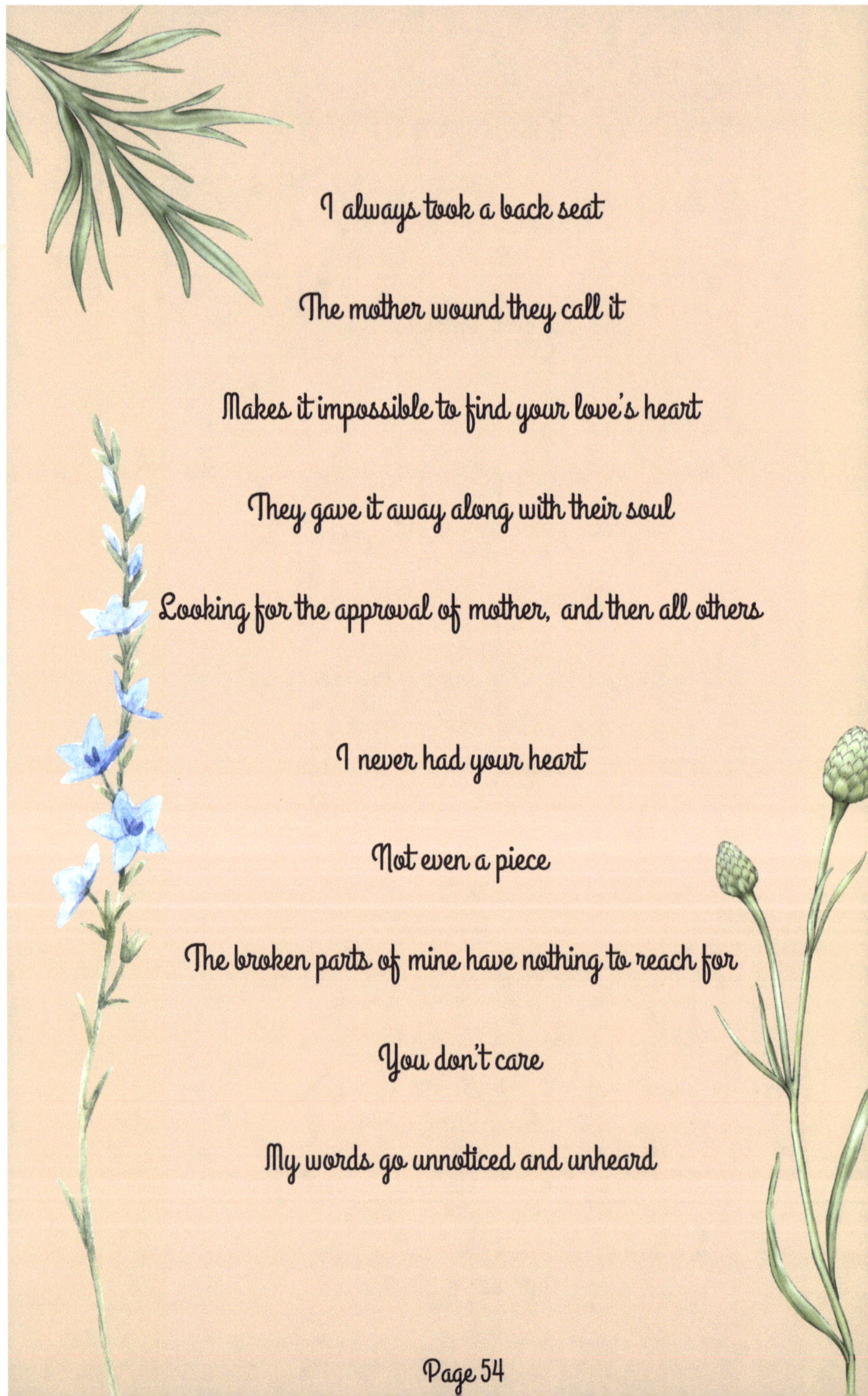

I always took a back seat

The mother wound they call it

Makes it impossible to find your love's heart

They gave it away along with their soul

Looking for the approval of mother, and then all others

I never had your heart

Not even a piece

The broken parts of mine have nothing to reach for

You don't care

My words go unnoticed and unheard

It feels like a game of Tetris

Yet the parts never come together

A man playing a part, but never feeling the role

And a bride left wondering why he never took her as his own

RIDE OR DIE

Bonnie is there for Clyde
Through thick and thin
Arrests
Job losses
Life's ups and downs
Getting her fired; his selfishness revealed
She ignores the negatives and only sees his gifts
Uplifts him always, gives her heart's energy to restore him
Insists he's great to counter his feelings of lack

Then Bonny and Clyde after escaping it all
Decide to have a child

Clyde decides he doesn't like the changes Bonnie goes through
He thinks that she "should" be the same person.

As if the changes were from her own accord; not the decision they both
made, one that took years of heartache to achieve

He can't see that his logic is irrelevant to her emotions
After bridging the worlds of Spirit and Earth
Bringing children and birthing a new version of herself alongside

Clyde seems to forget
He's also had new versions
After his arrests and defeats
After all the years hiding his feelings, like a pot boiling over
burning her on a daily basis

She accepts his new versions, as that is what unconditional love is.
She has no idea Clyde's love was that of a 'fairweather friend'

Bonnie shoulders the emotional burden and always uplifts him
Never says "you've changed" or demeans him
Giving him confidence
Nurturing him, loving him
Getting them to where they are today

The time she needs him is the time he decides
He was lying the whole time
He wanted her loyalty but can't truly be her "ride or die"

love you